Pablo

Picasso

Master of
Modern Art

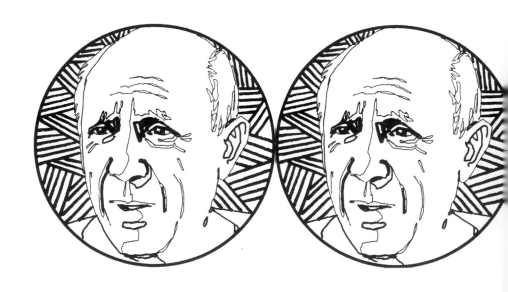

Pablo Picasso
Master of Modern Art

by Miranda Smith
illustrated by Harold Henriksen

Creative Education
Mankato, Minnesota 56001

Published by Creative Education, 123 South Broad Street,
P. O. Box 227, Mankato, Minnesota 56001
Copyright © 1974 by Creative Education. No part of this book may be reproduced
in any form without written permission from the publisher. International copyrights
reserved in all countries. Printed in the United States.
Distributed by Childrens Press. 1224 West Van Buren Street, Chicago, Illinois 60607

Library of Congress Numbers: 74-19319   ISBN: 0-87191-411-5

Library of Congress Cataloging in Publication Data
Smith, Miranda.   Pablo Picasso.
SUMMARY: A brief biography of one of the major artists of the
twentieth century considered the "father and master of modern art."
1. Picasso, Pablo, 1881-1973—Juvenile literature.
(1. Picasso, Pablo, 1881-1973.   2. Artists—France)
I. Henriksen, Harold, illus.   II. Title.
ND553.P5S57 759.4 (B) (92)   74-19319   ISBN 0-87191-411-5

INTRODUCTION

Pablo Picasso was one of the most fascinating men of our time. He was a great and innovative artist. He was a poet, playwright, comedian, and humanitarian.

Picasso loved life. He loved beautiful women, and several of them shared his life. Each woman inspired great new works of art. Their youth and beauty enabled Picasso to retain the freshness of his artistic vision.

Millions of people have prints of Picasso's work in their homes. His universal popularity made Picasso the wealthiest artist in history.

He was a genius, and geniuses are sometimes permitted everything. His long life is a story of adventure and fame, written by his paintings. Picasso's art is full of beauty, ugliness, youth, wisdom, fantasy, distortion, cruelty, and playfulness — as was his life.

Pablo Picasso

Master of
Modern Art

Picasso once said, "Reality is more than the thing itself. I always look for its super-reality. Reality lies in how you see things. A green parrot is also a green salad *and* a green parrot. He who makes it only a parrot diminishes its reality."

Pablo Picasso sought through his art to open our eyes. He wanted us to see that there is more than we *think* we see in things. Picasso's completely new approach to art has shocked many people. For years, he had to endure the ridicule which his brave experiments in painting received. But the laughter did not bother him.

Once when he saw an exhibition of children's drawings, Picasso remarked, "When I was their age, I could draw like Raphael; but it took me a lifetime to learn to draw like them." Picasso's seemingly crude style was the result of many years of hard work. His art education started off like that of most artists. But Picasso's insight sparked his discovery of countless possibilities in art. His vision sharpened and increased. His many revolutionary styles of painting reflected that vision.

Picasso's discoveries made a great impact on other artists. Suddenly they were free to give full rein to their imaginations. Painting changed drastically. Picasso was really the father and master of modern art.

"When I don't have blue, I use red." This remark of Picasso's demonstrates the playful side of his changeable

nature. He was at turns loving and self-centered, joyous and miserable, mature and child-like. His emotions were always hard to anticipate. As an admirer once said, "Nothing one can say about Picasso is exact."

Pablo Ruiz Picasso was born October 25, 1881, at Málaga, Spain. His father, José Ruiz Blasco, was a painter and the curator of the local museum. His mother, Maria Picasso Lopez, was of a prominent Málaga family. Pablo inherited from her his sparkling black eyes, short stature, and small, well-shaped hands.

Pablo made a very dramatic entrance into the world. The midwife who delivered him thought that he had been born dead. She put him aside and attended to his mother. Luckily, however, an uncle who was a doctor was present and saved Pablo's life by blowing air into his lungs. Picasso was on his way.

Pablo was given 14 names, those of relatives and saints, at his christening. Such is the tradition in Málaga. But he was just known as Pablo Ruiz Picasso. (In Spain, a child takes his mother's name in addition to his father's.) Later Pablo dropped the Ruiz and used only Picasso because it was such a distinctive name.

Picasso is not a typical Spanish name, and some people think that his mother's family was related to the 18th-century painter Matteo Picasso.

It is also said that there was gypsy blood in Picasso. Pablo always felt close to gypsies, and much of their passion and violence, sorrow and gaiety was to be found in him. A Spanish friend of Pablo's once said, "In the great nation of the gypsies of art, Picasso is the most gypsy of all."

Pablo developed extremely rapidly in his childhood. He drew before he could speak. His first words were "Piz, piz," a demand for "lapiz," which means "pencil" in Spanish. His father encouraged Pablo's drawing and taught him the fundamentals of art.

When Pablo was 10, his family moved to La Coruña, a rainy, foggy, isolated place in Spain very much unlike sunny Málaga. Pablo's father was forced to move there because he needed a better-paying job. Besides his own family, Don José had to support many other relatives. One of Pablo's sisters died soon after the move, and everyone hated La Coruña.

At La Coruña, Pablo spent most of his time sketching families at the beach or drawing portraits of his sister Lola. But Pablo hated school and did not do well there at all. He barely learned to read and couldn't remember how the alphabet went. Arithmetic was especially hard for him. He could not understand what numbers meant and could see in them only shapes which resembled birds and faces. He passed his examinations only because a teacher gave him all the answers.

That was all there was to Pablo's basic education. He devoted all his time to the study of art, tutored by his father.

Don José was a traditionally realistic painter, and most

of his paintings were of pigeons. Since his son had such advanced ability, Don José often had Pablo paint the feet of the pigeons in his pictures.

One evening he assigned this task to 13-year-old Pablo and went out for a walk, feeling sad and depressed about life in miserable La Coruña. When he returned, he realized that the pigeons' feet painted in by Pablo were much better than his own work. He gave his son all his materials and vowed that he would never paint again.

When Pablo was 14, the family moved to Barcelona. Don José took a post as a professor at the School of Fine Arts there. Pablo attended the School but was far too advanced for his class. He took the examination for entry to a higher level. Pablo astounded his examiners by completing the exam in one day. The test, which consisted of a drawing, usually took students one month. Pablo did much better in one day than the older students did in a month.

Don José found his son a studio nearby where he could work undisturbed. Pablo produced many fine paintings, but no one bought them. He was considered too young to be taken seriously.

In the fall of 1897, Pablo left home for the first time and went to Madrid. One of his uncles was paying Pablo's way to the Royal Academy of San Fernando. Once again, Pablo completed the examination in a day. At the amazing age of 16, he had passed all the academic tests of all the official Spanish art schools.

But Pablo hardly ever attended his classes at the Academy. He didn't feel he could learn anything there. Instead, he enjoyed life in the streets and in the cafés where artists met. His uncle did not like Pablo's behavior and cut off the money. But Pablo hardly cared; he enjoyed life even in poverty.

The next summer, however, Pablo became ill with scarlet fever and returned to his family in Barcelona. Later he accompanied a friend to the small village of Horta de San

Juan, where he learned farming and did a great deal of drawing. Sometimes when the heat was unbearable in the valley, the 2 young artists went up into the mountains and lived in a cave there, working in shady solitude.

In the spring of 1899 Pablo returned to Barcelona. He discovered new companions at a tavern called "The Four Cats," which was a hangout of painters, poets, and musicians. Pablo enjoyed listening for hours to these lively, exciting artists. They admired his talent and accepted him as one of their group. Pablo would sit quietly as the others spoke, drawing portraits of them.

It has been said that Picasso could close his eyes and with a single line draw perfect shapes of animals. He rarely did a portrait from a model. He had already memorized every feature of that person with his intense, penetrating gaze.

In the fall of 1900 Pablo made his first trip to Paris with a friend, Carlos Casagemas. Pablo felt he would conquer the great art capital at once. But there were hundreds of artists in Paris, and Picasso was conquered himself by cold and hunger. Casagemas was despairing over a hopeless love. The 2 friends returned to Barcelona in December.

Pablo's family found him changed; they thought him too ragged and unruly. He broke with them and went with Casagemas to Madrid. But Casagemas could not get over his unhappy love. He went back to Paris. Later Pablo heard that his friend had committed suicide.

Picasso was alone and unhappy in Madrid. But soon he met other artists. He and one of his new friends started a magazine called *Arte Joven (Young Art)*. They could not make enough money to publish many issues, but it had been a valuable experience for them.

In the spring of 1901 Pablo returned to Paris. He shared a room in a poor section with another artist. They barely survived, always cold and hungry but dreaming of fame and fortune.

In June, 75 of Picasso's paintings were exhibited. They were mostly cafe scenes with bright, vivid colors, influenced by other artists whom Pablo admired. Some people appreciated Picasso's work, but no one bought any of it.

Many artists and writers befriended Pablo in Paris. They were all poor but had a splendid time together. They would come to visit Pablo and see what he was doing, and he would go out with them to cafés. Everyone would drink, argue, and sing for hours. Finally Pablo would go home and start to work. He would work all night with great speed and concentration, and then sleep until the afternoon.

If anyone except those interested in buying paintings came to see him in the morning, Pablo would fly into a rage and chase the intruder away. His friends soon learned not to drop in on him until later in the day.

Picasso returned to Barcelona in January, 1902, but went back to Paris at the end of summer. He was not sure where he wanted to be. This time he lived with another artist in a small room which contained one big bed. There was so little space left over that one of them had to be in the bed if the other was in the room.

Pablo's very good friend Max Jacob was disturbed about this situation and invited Pablo to share his apartment, which was a little bigger. Max had only one small bed, so one of them worked while the other slept. Pablo was penniless and sometimes had to burn piles of drawings to keep warm.

Pablo returned once again to Barcelona in January, 1903. He was very restless and was trying to find just the right place to work. Pablo left Barcelona for Paris in April, 1904, for the last time. From then on he lived in France and was considered a French artist.

The paintings of these restless years (1901-1904) were of beggars and weary-looking workers with grave faces. A tired woman leaning on her iron, sad mothers with thin babies in their arms, and other scenes of misery and poverty filled the canvases. Nearly every painting was all blue in color. This is known as Picasso's Blue Period.

One day in 1904 Pablo met a girl at the well, used by the residents of the shabby building in which he lived. She was a sturdy 20-year-old with beautiful green eyes and brown hair. Picasso took Fernande Olivier to see his studio, and she stayed with him for many years.

Pablo was very jealous and did not allow Fernande out of the studio unless he went with her. She was quite content, though, to lie on a couch all day reading or listening to

PICASSO'S GANG

FERNANDE

BLUE PERIOD

GERTRUDE STEIN

him and a group of friends argue passionately about art. These artists were always at one another's throats, but in truth they enjoyed each other immensely and called themselves "Picasso's gang."

Pablo spent his days like this, but at night he was back at work. Since he usually could not afford oil for the lamp, he squatted in front of or leaned over his canvas with a candle in one hand and a brush in the other. He once said, "If a painting looks good in that light, it's sure to look good in daylight."

The floor was littered with tubes of paint and almost

everything else imaginable. Picasso saved everything but never put anything in order. He enjoyed the chaotic state of his living quarters. He thought that things were seen more clearly if they were out of their usual places. Pablo often hung pictures crooked for this reason.

Picasso's luck had begun to change. He was introduced to Leo and Gertrude Stein, well-known American patrons of the arts. They recognized Picasso's worth and bought several of his paintings.

This was very fortunate for Pablo because his pride no longer allowed him to exhibit his work or do illustrating jobs. He and Fernande had often nearly starved. At these times Fernande had been sent out to pawn her earrings.

Picasso's frequent visits to a circus outside Paris marked the beginning of a new style of painting. Pablo loved to watch the acrobats, clowns, and animals in their colorful setting. Graceful young figures mostly rose-pink in color now replaced the dreary beggars of the Blue Period. The years 1905 and 1906 when Picasso painted in this style, are know as the Rose Period.

Picasso was becoming well known. When he went to cafés, curious people would crowd around him, asking about the meaning of his work. Pablo detested explaining his paintings. He got a great deal of satisfaction at these times by pulling a revolver out of his pocket and firing a few shots into the air. The foolish admirers scattered immediately.

Pablo went often to visit Gertrude and Leo Stein. At their apartment he met many fascinating characters, including Henri Matisse, who was to become Pablo's greatest friend in later years. It was inevitable that he would absorb new ideas from all these brilliant artists.

One day Pablo went to an exhibit of African art in a damp, musty museum basement. He felt sick to his stomach from the stench, but the grimacing African masks caught his attention. He stayed there for hours, fascinated. The African objects were considered only curiosities. But Pablo had made a discovery. These grotesque faces were actually another culture's concept of beauty.

In 1907 Picasso painted *The Ladies of Avignon*. Five nudes stare out from the canvas, their bodies twisted unnaturally. The faces of 2 of the women are striped and savage, like African masks. No painting like this had ever been done before. Pablo's friends were shocked at his strange picture and thought he had lost his mind. But Picasso knew that this was a great step forward in his work.

Friends stopped coming to see Pablo. But he continued to paint in the same way, excited by the new style. It was the first time Picasso was completely himself and not influenced by other artists.

Finally Georges Braque, one of Pablo's closest friends, admitted that there was something to Picasso's idea. The 2 artists carried the new style on to what became known as cubism. In a cubist painting, everyday objects are formed by masses of geometric shapes. Cubism was a whole new way of looking at things.

The public was stunned. But shock gave way to curiosity, and Picasso's paintings began to be bought again, more than ever.

With his new riches, Pablo moved with Fernande into a bigger apartment in a better section of Paris. He bought paintings, furniture, and African objects. He went to the countryside in summer. And he kept on working.

In 1912 Picasso and Fernande's life together ended. He had become tired of her, and they often fought. As soon as Fernande left, a friend of hers filled her place. She was a delicate, gentle girl named Eva Gouel.

"I love her very much, and I shall write her name on my pictures," Pablo declared. Eva inspired many fine cubist paintings by Picasso. The words "Ma Jolie" ("My Pretty One") were printed on these paintings, as a dedication to her.

Picasso went to a villa in Avignon for the spring and summer. There he continued to paint, and even drew on the walls of the villa. He often did this, and once a landlord made Pablo pay for the repainting of a wall. Picasso said later, "What a fool. He could have sold the whole wall for a fortune if he had only had the sense to leave it." Pablo liked the drawing on the wall of the Avignon villa so much that he cut out the section he liked and took it back to Paris.

Picasso had few real admirers at this stage of cubism, but one faithful defender, the poet Guillaume Apollinaire, said of Pablo, "his insistence on the pursuit of beauty has since changed everything in art."

The First World War broke out in 1914, and many of Pablo's friends went off to fight. Pablo was lonely and sad, but he ignored the war and continued to paint.

Few paintings were done in 1915. Eva died after a long illness; Pablo was heartbroken and even more alone.

Picasso continued his experiments with cubism. In 1917 he was asked to help design costumes and scenery for the Russian Ballet. Pablo worked with enthusiasm on this new adventure, creating cubist costumes out of which only the legs of the dancers appeared. The ballet was received with shock and anger. The artists were nearly attacked by the outraged audience.

But Pablo's involvement in the ballet was not a total loss. He met Olga Koklova, one of the Russian ballerinas, and married her in 1918.

Olga was the daughter of an upper-class family and was used to living well. Picasso was captivated by the idea of "the good life." He and Olga moved into an elegant new apartment. Pablo dressed extravagantly and went to fashionable parties with Olga. In 1921 they had a son and called him Paulo.

Picasso's style of painting kept changing. In the 1920's he painted many pictures of massive women. He did bright, colorful cubist paintings and sculpture. Once Picasso was asked if he always knew what a finished painting would look like. Pablo answered, "When you work, you don't know what is going to come out of it. It is not indecision; the fact is it changes while you are at work."

Pablo continued to visit his friends to see what they were doing. But the other artists weren't very glad to see him when they were in their studios. They would hide their latest work when he came because they feared Picasso would steal an idea of theirs and do it better. Pablo himself used to say, "If there's anything to steal, I steal."

For the next 10 years Picasso continued to progress as an artist. The family spent summers in Spain or in the south of France. Often they went to the Mediterranean coast. Pablo loved a hot, sunny climate and worked well in that environment.

But Picasso was not happy. Life with Olga did not suit him anymore. She was too demanding, and Pablo was tired of the ridiculous "high life" she wanted. He could not divorce Olga because of Spanish law, so they separated.

In 1932 Pablo met a lovely young woman named Marie-Thérèse Walter. For a long time her classic, serene face dominated Picasso's bright, peaceful paintings of women. She and Pablo had a daughter, Maïa, in 1935.

Now Pablo decided to try his hand at another art form — poetry. He found grammar and punctuation difficult, so he dispensed with them and wrote very free-form verse in

Spanish. It won quite a bit of acclaim. In 1941 Pablo also wrote a play called *Desire Caught by the Tail*. It was much like his poetry, full of fantasy and color.

Picasso met the beautiful and intelligent Dora Maar in 1936. She was a photographer and painter who knew many of his friends. Here was a woman with whom he could talk about art, in Spanish as well as French. Pablo's love of Dora inspired many beautiful, soft portraits of her in the early phase of their companionship. But Dora's lovely face became grave and tormented as time passed and the war came. She became the "weeping woman" of Picasso's paintings, which turned grim and tortured with strife.

Picasso was commissioned to do a mural for the Spanish Pavilion at the World's Fair in Paris. This painting was to be one of the landmarks of his career. The subject matter of the painting was determined by the April 26, 1937, destruction of the Spanish town of Guernica. Hundreds of innocent people were killed in the German bombing. This act of horror so angered Picasso that he painted his masterpiece *Guernica* in response. Ever since its creation, Guernica has stood as a condemnation of the brutality of war.

The Second World War began in 1939. Picasso was in Antibes, in the south of France. He was worried about the huge collection of drawings and paintings he had left in Paris. Pablo feared it might be destroyed by the Nazis, who denounced his work. Despite the possibility of being captured by the Nazis, he returned to Paris in 1940 and remained there for the rest of the war.

The Germans did not bother Picasso because they were afraid of criticism from other nations. Instead, they attempted to win Picasso to their side with gifts of food and other privileges. Pablo refused all of their offers. He hated what the Nazis stood for, and lived through the war with little fuel and food.

After the Liberation of Paris in 1944, people around the world were wondering if Picasso was still alive. There had been no news of him during the German Occupation. When the first Americans came into Paris, they rushed eagerly to Pablo's studio to see if he was all right. There he was, painting away.

The world was relieved and overjoyed. Picasso suddenly became the symbol of man fighting injustice. His studio was constantly crammed with American soldiers who considered Picasso the greatest Parisian landmark after the Eiffel Tower. Pablo barely found time to work with the continuous flow of visitors.

Now Picasso decided to become a member of the Communist Party. Many artists and intellectuals had joined, believing that communism was the only way to stop wars. They thought that communism could form a just and humane society.

Although the Communists did not approve of Picasso's art, he did not change it. He said, "My adhesion to the Communist Party is the logical outcome of my whole life.

... I have wanted, by drawing and by color, since those were my weapons, to penetrate always further forward into the consciousness of the world and of men.... These years of terrible oppression have proved to me that I should struggle not only for my art but with my whole being."

Many people objected to Picasso's painting at this time, partly because he was a Communist, and partly because they just couldn't understand his work. There were near-riots at some of his exhibitions. But Picasso explained his painting this way: "I want to draw the mind in a direction it's not used to and wake it up. I want to help the viewer discover something he wouldn't have discovered without me."

In 1943 Picasso met a girl named Françoise Gilot. Pablo was 61; Françoise was 21. She came often to his studio to discuss art, and he would show her his work and instruct her in painting, which was her main interest. Françoise brought Picasso much happiness. His joy is apparent in the portraits he did of her. Pablo painted Françoise as a delicate yet strong flower or as the sun. There is a gentleness in these portraits which was quite new to his work.

Françoise later wrote a fascinating book about him called *Life with Picasso.* In it, she recounted many of his unusual traits which were unknown to most of the world. Picasso became even more of a household word. His secrets were revealed.

Françoise's description of him presents an interesting picture. Picasso was quite small, only 5-feet-3 inches, but very muscular. Everyone who met him said that the most notable thing about him was his eyes. They were very black, bright, and intense, and seemed to look right through everything.

Pablo was very superstitious, or perhaps just enjoyed superstitions because they were amusing. He was playful. One of his favorite pastimes was blowing on a bugle several times a day.

He also loved children and animals. He kept many birds,

including turtledoves, pigeons, and owls, which would perch on his shoulder. He had cats, dogs, and a couple of goats, and he let them roam freely throughout the house.

Picasso hated airplanes, haircuts, and dancing. He found only one barber, a Spaniard, whom he trusted. After cutting Pablo's hair, the barber would take the clippings and deposit them in a secret place. Pablo loved these little mysteries.

Picasso never went to his exhibition openings and usually refused to explain his work. He hated getting new clothes and usually wore very old ones full of holes. If he were forced to buy a new suit, he'd put it away in a closet for months. When he finally went to wear it, it was moth-eaten and shabby like his other clothes.

Françoise says that Picasso was always in a black mood when he woke up, which was usually around noon. It would take her hours to convince him that life was all right, that everyone loved him and that he was a genius. Consoled at last, Pablo would get up, feeling fine.

He would not make simple decisions, such as whether or not he would go to the bullfights, so others had to make them for him. The decisions that were made were always what he really wanted. But if he was at all unhappy about the outcome, he would heap the blame for his discomfort on those around him.

Life with Picasso must have been difficult at times, as Françoise pointed out, but there were good times, too. Pablo and Françoise had 2 children whom Pablo loved very much

— Claude, born in 1947, and Plaoma, born in 1949. Picasso and his family were often to be found romping on a Mediterranean beach.

There was an old pottery factory in the southern French town of Vallauris, where Picasso had bought a pink villa. Pablo decided to give ceramics a try. He turned out vases and jugs shaped like women, birds and heads. He painted on pots and plates and made lovely doves out of clay. The result of his labors in the factory was yet another proof that Picasso could extract beautiful new possibilities from an old art.

Another venture Picasso embarked upon at this time was the decorating of an old chapel in Vallauris. Pablo locked himself in the chapel and came out only to eat and sleep. After 2 months the huge painting *War and Peace* was finished. It was done very rapidly yet brilliantly, as was typical of Picasso's work.

Picasso produced over 20,000 objects in his lifetime, including drawings, paintings, sculptures, and ceramics. Another Picasso production was the "readymade," which consisted of objects which he found. He assembled the objects into a sculpture or they just stood alone, untouched, as sculpture. An example of a "readymade" is Picasso's *Bull* which consists of a pair of bicycle handlebars and a bicycle seat put together to look like a bull's head.

Picasso's incredible output was the result of his drive and extremely fast work. When he felt puzzled by something

he was working on, he put it aside with the thousands of other pieces lying around and picked up something else.

Pablo once said, "Pictures are never finished in the sense that they suddenly become ready to be signed and framed. They usually come to a halt when the time is ripe because something happens which breaks the continuity of their development. . . . After all, a work of art is not achieved by thought but with your hands."

Françoise found that life with Picasso was not working out. She felt that the man, great as he was, was very self-centered and lived solely for his art. Françoise left Picasso in 1953 and took the children with her. Pablo was indignant that anyone should leave him and was a little sorry, too, to see her go. But he wasn't alone for long.

Jacqueline Roque came to live with him and take care of the "old man," now 72 years old. She was the last in the long line of lovely women who shared Picasso's life.

Olga, Pablo's first wife, died in 1955. Jacqueline and Picasso were married in 1961. Jacqueline, a quiet, gentle woman, devoted herself to making Pablo's life pleasant. She was always at his side, keeping him company while he painted.

The public still clamored for Picasso, but now there were barbed-wire fences around his estates. Pablo received only a few visitors. He was still very healthy and youthful, but he was afraid of dying before he had done all he wanted to do. His work of the last years is full of soft, bright colors. He did new variations on the old themes of bullfights, matadors, and a woman's face — now Jacqueline's.

Picasso kept working until he died suddenly of a heart attack on April 8, 1973. He was 91. Picasso died the most widely known artist in the world and probably in all of history as well. The passionate genius, the fun-loving millionaire, the great figure of the 20th century, was gone. But Picasso's art will live on for centuries to come.

Miranda Smith

This is Miranda Smith's first published book. She is currently working on a fantasy for children and translations of French children's stories.

At the University of Minnesota she took courses in art and foreign languages. In addition to French, Miranda has studied Latin, Italian, Portuguese, and Russian. Among her other interests are drawing, sailing, and traveling.

Miranda lives in Minneapolis, Minnesota, with her husband Jay and daughter Zoë. Jay H. Smith has written 10 books for children, 7 of which have been published by Creative Education.

Harold Henriksen

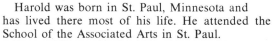

Harold was born in St. Paul, Minnesota and has lived there most of his life. He attended the School of the Associated Arts in St. Paul.

Even while serving in the Army, Harold continued to keep alive his desire to become an artist. In 1965 he was a winner in the All Army Art Contest.

After the Army, Harold returned to Minnesota where he worked for several art studios in the Minneapolis-St. Paul area. In 1967 he became an illustrator for one of the largest art studios in Minneapolis.

During 1971 Harold and his wife traveled to South America where he did on-the-spot drawings for a year. Harold, his wife and daughter Maria now live in Minneapolis where he works as a free lance illustrator.

close ups

Walt Disney
Bob Hope
Duke Ellington
Dwight Eisenhower
Coretta King
Pablo Picasso
Ralph Nader
Bill Cosby
Dag Hammarskjold
Sir Frederick Banting
Mark Twain
Beatrix Potter